# *My Beloved, Gyuri*

a story of resilience

## ROBERTA RABINEK

# MY BELOVED GYURI

## A STORY OF RESILIENCE

### FIRST EDITION

Roberta Rabinek

© 2021 Roberta Rabinek

First Edition

Hope Publishing

My Beloved Gyuri: A Story of Resilience

Printed in the United States of America
Print ISBN: 978-1-66780-523-8

*To our children and grandchildren*
*And the strong survival instinct within us all*

# Contents

# *Introduction*

He never died. I still hear his voice—the beautiful Hungarian accent of Gyuri* (George) Rabinek, my second husband. He says my name "Roberta" and the "R's" roll romantically in the recess of my mind. I feel his presence as the leaves turn to exquisite hues of golds, reds, and oranges, as the strains of Mozart suddenly flow through a radio, as a museum's Vincent van Gogh painting catches my eye.

His dry wit is a constant reminder of who he was. I hear his uproarious laughter as I reply "yes" we will share our lives together. Loud laughter was not, for him, a frequent occurrence. Gyuri lived through torturous times; he survived a nightmare. Still, he was brave, open-minded, optimistic, and realistic.

He had a sense of purpose, a strong sense of ethics and a wry sense of humor. The world is better for the grace of his existence. Through his life story and the tale of a dark period of history, along with his indomitable will to live and his positivity—readers, his family, and all those to come, will hopefully be inspired to find their own purposes in life.

*Gyuri is pronounced Jury*

1

*Lost*

My childhood innocence

Forever

My lightheartedness

Forever gone.

Darkness in my soul

Forever there.

Amidst the laughter

Amidst the joy

Forever there.

By Roberta Rabinek

To my husband, Gyuri Rabinek

2nd of June 1992

# The Café

Everything about Gyuri Rabinek intrigued me. One evening we were sitting in the small café for several hours. Around us the waiter was mopping the floor, the cashier was counting out the register, and the candle at our table was burning low. Gyuri took a deep breath, leaned back in his chair, and I reached across the table to touch his hand. I was speechless. Gyuri had related a riveting tale.

It was our third date and I had asked, "What were your experiences in Hungary during the Nazi occupation?"

His reply surprised me. "No one has ever asked me that question."

And with that, his story began.

*In Gyuri's Own Words*

In late spring 1942, my class matriculated from high school. When the class work was finished, we marched down the corridors of the Jewish *Gymnazium* in Budapest, Hungary, singing farewell to our lower classmates. They stood along the corridor walls as we sang, "Gaudeamus igitur juvenes dum sumus…" [By Hungarian composer Franz Liszt. It means "Let us rejoice therefore while we are young after a pleasant youth…" This is a popular, well-known student song written in 1781.] For us, this was an emotionally touching experience.

Public displays of hatred against Jews took place in the last few years of our *gymnazium* life. One day in 1941, a mob attacked our *gymazium* building. A large group of graduates from the school rushed to our defense, protecting us and the building. We were required to wear school caps identifying us as Jewish high school students. As a result, it was not safe for us to walk alone to school; we always formed a group in order to avoid attacks. After graduation, as Jews, we did not have a chance to pursue higher education.

An anti-Jewish law passed in prior years took care of this. Unable to continue school, I went to work in a small factory fabricating foot-operated machines used by dentists. I learned to use metal fabrication equipment such as drills and files. After spending two years at that place, I do not remember anything but frustration and monotony, week after week.

In March 1944, the German allies of Hungary marched into our country and occupied it. Governor Nicholas Horthy's power had no teeth. [Horthy was the regent of Hungary from World War I through World War II (March 20, 1920-October 15, 1944.)] More anti-Jewish laws were declared.

We were forced to wear a yellow star on our lapels, Jews could not own a business, and my father's textile material store was taken away.

My father and I were directed at different times to report to military groups. Like other Jews in our country, we were put into forced labor troops but did not get to have weapons. I had to go to Fulek, a small town in northern Hungary. *Apu*'s troop had to unload ships in Budapest. Nevertheless, we were lucky we were not used for military work connected to army barracks in Eastern Europe, for many of the workers there were brutally murdered. Hay Andor, my *gymnazium* schoolmate, was one of the workers eliminated there.

Even through mail with our family, we had no idea about the war's progress. My two friends, Lieberman Endre and Lowi Gyuri [last name, first name—Hungarian style], were in my troop. Their families lived outside Budapest and were deported to the Polish concentration camps. Suddenly my two friends stopped getting mail.

Thankfully I remained in touch with my astute mother, who was aware of important happenings in the Jewish community. She was able to get a *schutzpass*, distributed by the Swiss embassy, for every member of our family. These papers saved our lives on several occasions. [Early on Gyuri was deported to concentration camps; the same with his mother and two sisters. They let them all go back because they all had a *schutzpass*. But later on, Gyuri was deported anyway.]

In November 1944, the Arrowcross Party, a Nazi party, governed Hungary, murdering Jews with hateful brutality. They were the ones who led groups to the shores of the Danube River and shot them to die in the icy water. My mother and sisters were in one of the hundreds of groups forced to march toward a concentration camp in Austria. Their first night's stop was at a brick-making kiln. Those with a *shutzpass* were separated from the others and marched back to Budapest. *Anu* and my sisters were fortunate....

May to September 1944, my forced labor group worked in Fulek. We were excavating an old fortress destroyed by the Turks a couple hundred years earlier. We excavated the exterior stone walls and the rampart on top. After a while, we enjoyed the work. We found utensils, iron cannon balls, remains of building walls, and the ceramic facing of a large masonry oven. I found all the broken pieces to a picturesque ceramic panel showing a *fuleki hussar*, a Hungarian soldier on horseback. This was a major find for the Hungarian Arrowcross archeologist. For a reward, I received an escorted trip home to Budapest for a few days.

In Budapest, we still had our shortwave radio. And on *Apu's* birthday, which was D-day, the BBC told us the great news that English and American troops landed on the shores of Europe.

In September, our forced labor troop was ordered to march south toward the Danube. When we reached the river, the guys with a *schutzpass*, like the one I had, were marched to a military barracks in Budapest. The others, including my two friends, were force marched to a concentration camp in Austria. All of us were tired from the long starvation marches and we were filled with apprehension about what was coming next.

The next day, those in my group were marched to Ercsi, a small town south of Budapest on the western shore of the Danube. Our journey ended in a sugar factory where we slept during the day and where we worked at night digging trenches along the edge of the river in complete silence. We were told the Russian army was on the other shore of the river, and if the Russians saw or heard people moving around, they would shoot.

Approximately two weeks later, we were awakened in the morning and directed to march quickly away from the river. Everyone was moving at a fast pace. The Hungarian soldiers sped away and other people followed quickly. Suddenly we were isolated. Four of us decided to slow down. We thought we would let the Russians liberate us. The yellow star on our jackets would show we were oppressed by the Hungarians. Undoubtedly, we felt, the Russians would liberate us.

As the war was ending, we realized that falling into Russian hands would be extremely dangerous, for the Russians were brutal and indiscriminate.

Women who were liberated were raped repeatedly. Others were robbed and mistreated.

We were alone on the road and suddenly a Russian plane swooped down and machine-gunned us. We rolled into the ditch on the side of the road, then hid beside haystacks and waited. After a few hours, the situation changed. Hungarian soldiers returned, heading back toward the river. We were arrested by the country police and taken to the police yard. Our situation looked bad, for the gypsies who were also pushed into this yard did not want to be grouped with us. We were saved by an air raid as English planes bombarded the neighborhood.

We were taken to our labor troop and the next day started a march back to Budapest. Hungarian soldiers robbed us during the march, taking all our jewelry, rings and everything in our pockets. It was memorable, for as we walked through a village, I saw how a locked-up Jewish house was opened with a key by some official, and he handed batches of clean linens to the neighbors. Our Jewish brothers and sisters were deported months earlier from this place and were, most likely, starving or dead in Polish concentration camps, robbed of all possessions.

We marched back to the military barracks in Budapest, in shock about our desperate situation. It was unbelievable, and it turned even worse in a few days.

I did not know what it meant to be driven into cattle wagons. When we, men and women in the barracks, were forced into groups and marched to a railroad station, I had strong apprehensions. I wrote a card to my mother at our home address and asked a passerby to mail it. I was forced into a cattle wagon—an empty box filled with lots of us Jews. We traveled two weeks in it.

Our situation as defenseless slaves became apparent very fast. Armed German soldiers surrounded the train and a few yells of demands came our way. We sat in a tight spot on the floor, touching somebody on every side. Starvation and thirst tortured us. I remember one night when for hours voices in the train were yelling *wásser* [water]. Otherwise deadly silence filled the wagon. When someone had to eliminate, he or she asked for the small metal cooking pot and had to bare his or her butt. Then the pot was passed to the individual sitting under the high ventilation opening so he could throw out the contents. There was neither toilet paper nor water with which to wash. And there was no medical help. A diabetic man sat next to me; he died the third day.

The train stopped frequently for many hours, sometimes for days. On one occasion we were told to get out in the countryside close to the Danube. Some of the women asked to walk over to the river to wash themselves, but they were not allowed. We had to stand as a tight group. I remember a few young guys ran away and were shot dead and left there. A few days later, all the women were evacuated and put into another wagon [cattle car].

We were very weak and worn out from desperation and starvation when we arrived at Buchenwald. It must have been around Christmas time, for two converted guys in our wagon, for some reason I can't understand, were humming Christmas carols. They must have lost their minds.

When we were commanded to leave the cattle wagons in the evening, many crawled weakly on the ground and some did not make it. Soon the large open ground area was covered with our Jewish brothers sitting or lying beside their packages. The barbed wire fence enclosure and the gate were visible in the distance. A few of us, young guys who knew each other from the Ercsi forced labor troop, sat together and decided to wait as long as we could.

I still had my Rabinek grandfather's ring baked into a stone hard muffin; I dug a hole and buried it into the clay ground. Then I got lucky. Kohn Feri, my cousin's brother-in-law, shuffled by and recognized me. He pointed out abandoned packages lying around. Why not look at the contents and search for food? We found many edibles and filled our bellies with smoked ham and other amazing food. This was my largest meal for about a year.

We were the last ones pushed through the gate into the Buchenwald camp. Our degradation continued with the stripping and taking of every stitch of our clothing, plus the shaving of our hair and collection of it. Then a bunch of *häftlings* [slaves] poked their unwashed dirty fingers in every hole of our bodies looking for valuables to find and take. It was a bitterly cold winter and we were on a hilltop wearing the flimsy striped cotton wear and wooden shoes given to us.

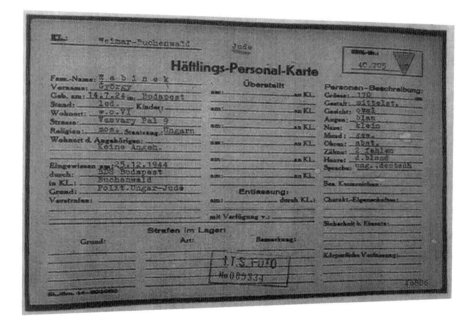

My jacket had an insignia identifying me as a Jew and showing my number—12854, which replaced my name. [After the war, Gyuri assumed he was not tattooed because he came into the camps close to the end of the war. "I don't know why my number wasn't tattooed," he said. "I didn't even know they had tattooed people. But the murdering continued."]

We were marched to our assigned barracks, surrounded with a barbed wire fence; it had a gate to the fence and an armed soldier guarded the enclosed latrine. The bunks around all the walls of the barracks had four levels of decking. This entire sleeping surface was hardly enough; the first night I could only sleep on my side. There was no room to turn. In the morning we were dished some brownish warm water, midday a ladleful of warm water with bits of turnip or such, and in the evening we received one slice of so-called bread.

The worst part of the day was late afternoon when we had to stand for hours in the bitter cold for the *Appell* [Appellplatz in German means roll call, or counting of the slaves] when our numbers were called and we had to shout *Ja* [German for "yes" and pronounced "yah"]. I still remember the latrine, which consisted of a long, deep 10 foot concrete ditch with long round poles as seats on both sides. There was nothing for the staggering famished users to hold onto. If someone fell in, that was the end. Looking at the exposed bottoms, I saw skin on bones.

A week or two later I could turn over lying down at night; many must have died and thus made room. Every day, throughout the day, we saw two slaves carrying a dead body. Thinking about the missing from our barracks, we assumed they could not get up for the *Appell*, and were carried out when we were at the assembly.

One morning I was assigned by the slave leader of our barracks to bring the bowl of brown water from the kitchen. When we got back, I figured I would take my portion while it was still hot. Was that a mistake! The slave leader beat me and did not stop punching until I threw myself on the ground. I still remember that beating.

All of a sudden, some of us got a lucky break. If we had any tool mechanic experience, we could volunteer to go to another place. We were surrounded with death, covered with dirt, and in a hopeless situation. So Peter Schlesinger and I volunteered. I started to talk to Peter the first day in Buchenwald when I looked around to find a familiar face in our barracks; I discovered he was the brother of a guy I knew quite well. We stuck together until our liberation and some time afterward.

It must have been the first week of January 1945 when we were loaded into cattle cars and traveled two days to Neubrandenburg. During this ride the SS guards lit a wood fire and most of us got close to passing out from the carbon monoxide fumes.

I remember puking through the gap in the slightly open sliding doors. I got a glimpse of the lit up city the evening we arrived at a factory; it had a fenced-off area as a concentration camp for us slaves. When I think about it today, and compare this camp with the many others where daily mass butchery and extermination went on during those days, I realize I was lucky.

This location was better than Buchenwald; we were not exposed to the cold weather when working and even the *Appells* were held indoors. The factory was not manufacturing anything; maybe there was no raw material. Our work was maintenance so we mixed mortar, laid block walls, and painted walls. I remember standing on a ladder for many days. I could hardly lift the pail of paint, the starvation showed in my dizziness. The *kapos* [special prisoners chosen by the Nazi SS camp guards to help run the camps and manage other prisoners] were Poles and they pushed us around. One who walked under my ladder got a pail of paint dropped on his head. I got away with a terrific beating.

Our camp had Dutch, Belgian, Polish, Ukrainian, and Hungarian Jewish slaves, about three hundred people. We were lucky to have a washroom; water was available for drinking and rinsing parts of our bodies. We also used the washroom to strip off our clothes in order to kill the lice from our garments and ourselves. This was the room where I got surrounded and attacked by a batch of young Ukrainian kids. I backed into a corner and prepared to defend myself. I fought them off until a few Dutch acquaintances came to my aid. The confrontation started earlier that day. These kids cornered and pushed around a staggering older Hungarian Jewish man and I pushed them away from him without giving it a thought.

We were stinking dirty, wearing the same dirty linen outfits we had on since the first day of slavery. The starvation must have altered our body functions; our hair, beard, and nails did not grow and we were dizzy and dragging ourselves. Peter worked in an office area so we had some paper for our butts. One time the leader of our slave group got hold of three carrots. He threw them up in the air to see the crowd of slaves fight for them. I caught one and shared it with Peter.

In the factory, we had to sign in by hanging a metal piece stamped with our number on a board of nails. I kept this piece of metal as a memento and it is in my cabinet today. The Poles and Ukrainians showed their anti-Semitism even in common slavery. I related to the Dutch and Belgian slaves and we tried to communicate in English. The fact that I tried to learn new English words showed my hidden optimism. The strangest thing that came about was when a member of the Polish group approached and asked me to teach the group English words. I can say I taught English in the concentration camp!

It must have been in April that the command came for all Jews to assemble and leave the camp, which projected the end of our lives was near. We were loaded onto an open truck and many hours later were pushed into Ravensbrück concentration camp. We arrived resigned, helpless and frightened.

In the yard we found tremendous piles of dead bodies, skins and bones, tightly packed about 10 feet high, 50 feet wide, and several hundred feet long. This sight hit us hard! But after many hours we did not see any SS soldiers and there was no order, no *Appell*. We were served the usual meager foodstuff. We did not see anything that looked immediately frightening. But who knew what could happen the next minute?

Now, many decades later after reading about all that happened in the last month of the Second World War, I am amazed at my unbelievable good luck. When the Allied Forces got near the concentration camps, the routine seems to have been a forced deadly march of the slaves to another concentration camp, or a brutal murder of them. When I read the Allies occupied Ravensbrück only a couple days after we arrived there, I realized we arrived too late to be cremated.

The next day we were packed tightly into cattle wagons to take us north to Wöbbelin concentration camp near Ludwigslust. But before we left, each one of us received a package of American canned food labeled *Fur die Juden* [For the Jews]. The Nazis probably figured the Allies could overtake us and our packages would help the Nazis look less inhuman. We held the food cans tightly, but could not eat any of it except for a few bites of the chocolate.

Two days later, our train filled with stinking dirty, starving slaves arrived with these U.S. packages. We were pushed into an unfinished barracks, which had masonry walls and a roof, but no floor, doors, or windows. We slept sitting on the clay ground, leaning against each other. One morning we found a member of our leaning-together bodies was dead. When I had to go to the latrine, I gave all my canned food to Peter to guard. If we stepped out of our barracks, we were attacked.

The kitchen was managed by Greek guys. One of them came to me to get a can of my margarine. We communicated in English and struck a deal. Next day Peter and I sat on the kitchen floor and dined, eating warm fish and bread but we could only eat a few bites. Our stomachs must have shrunk due to starvation.

One late afternoon we were herded into cattle cars, with *kapos* randomly beating many of us slaves. I noticed the beaten ones fell and were left on the ground. We were pushed into the wagons so tightly we could only stand. The tight push on all sides kept us from sliding to the floor. I managed to try and sit down but the tremendous stink between the bodies stopped me. We stood all night.

In the morning the wagon door opened and we walked back to our barracks. Apparently there was no engine or any camp to which they could take us. The slaves who fell when struck the night before lay dead on the ground. After a while we noticed the armed soldiers were not at their posts in the guard towers. They had disappeared!

We sat on the ground waiting to find out what was going on. Hours later a single jeep driven by two soldiers in strange uniforms drove into the camp, stopped, looked around and left. A short time later, another jeep drove in and we were told we were free. An amazing thing took place—the shuffling skeletons got filled with a new spark. A group started singing the Greek national anthem and everybody just stood; then came the singing of the Polish anthem as well as the singing of a few others. Then we ex-Hungarian Jews sang the "Hatikvah" as well as we remembered it. I felt deeply uplifted singing it and seeing all the other skeletal figures just standing around us in silence. [Both before and during the war, Hungary was a fascist nation that practiced anti-Semitism; so Hungarian Jews in the camps sang "Hatikvah" instead of the Hungarian National anthem. Gyuri felt Jews weren't really Hungarian because the Hungarians were so bad to the Jews. Once he came to this country, he viewed himself as completely American.]

On the day of our liberation we did not celebrate. We felt the joy of having survived but were busy dealing with our new situation. A lot of activity went on in the campsite as the liberated slaves tore into some storage structures. On the one hand this was great for we managed to obtain some food. I vaguely recall cooking some cereal. But on the other hand, we felt threatened seeing groups of people with firearms shooting in the air. We remembered we were attacked the previous days for our canned food, and we still had a few cans.

A group of us, ex-Hungarian Jewish guys, decided to be very cautious and we spent the first night of liberation in an abandoned cattle wagon away from the crowd. And in the morning, we left the camp. We started to walk to find a place where we could settle down peacefully.

From Liberation to Arrival in
the U.S.

The day after liberation we started walking away from Wöbbelin concentration camp. We passed a broken down motorcycle with abandoned clothing on it. I remember taking some clothing and throwing away my lice-infested items. When we got to a highway heading to the town of Schwerin, we kept on walking slowly. Suddenly some U.S. troops passed by and a GI newspaper on the pavement had the headline: *President Roosevelt is dead.*

After a while we got hungry and tried to persuade a local German farmer to give us a little food, but to no avail. I went over to a U.S. soldier and asked if he could convince that same German farmer to give us food. The Americans stormed into the house with guns drawn, telling them to prepare a banquet and pointing to us. Consequently we got a large meal of egg omelets with salami and bread! Then we kept walking.

I remember arriving at Schwerin airport, which was occupied by U.S. troops. At the airport a large barbed wire enclosure for German soldiers was surrounded by many GI guards. We were looking for an outfit that would help us. But there was no such group, no Red Cross. I approached a U.S. sergeant and explained our problem— we were liberated Jews and didn't know where to go.

This was our first conversation with an American, and this man, Leo Etter, is memorable to me even today, sixty-two years later. He arranged for us to get leftover food from the soldiers' meals and showed us an empty building where we could settle. After that day, Leo was a daily visitor to our place. He was an intelligent caring man filled with goodwill for us. He came alone to chat, mainly with me, as the other boys did not speak English. Often other soldiers came with him. I distinctly remember GI's sitting around our place with their boots on the table; their informality impressed me. The GI's asked about our experiences and our past. They talked about America too and that was of extreme interest to me.

*In July 1945, this troop of soldiers left Germany; the troop was scheduled to join the war against the Japanese forces. Leo kept in touch with me and when I arrived to the United States, he surprised me. He had arranged for me to go to his hometown, Harrisburg, Pennsylvania. Leo planned to present me with generous support from the Jewish community. I would be able to start a new life. Unfortunately my sickness needed attention at that time and I landed in a hospital in Denver, Colorado.*

*In later years, I visited Leo several times. Subsequently he was afflicted with an illness, which confined him to his house where he lived with his wife. When he died a few years later, I went to his funeral with my son Robert.*

The Schwerin airfield where we lived became a displaced persons' camp and it had a large kitchen. The ten of us did not like the food. I remember peeling potatoes day after day and living on mashed potatoes for a long time. We rested, ate, and slowly recovered our strength. In August 1945, British troops occupied our area of Germany. Shortly thereafter they asked us whether we wanted to go with them to West Germany as they said the Schwerin area would shortly be occupied by Russian troops. We kept hearing bad news about the treatment of survivors under Russian occupation. So we got on the train to travel west.

Our group ended up in the town of Lüneburg. We did not want to just sit around in a displaced persons' camp so four of us found work at the British Air Force officers building. In the morning we served them tea. I remember working in the kitchen. During the officers' social hour we serve them drinks. Our tent was set up next to the officers' building. We acquired a taste for English tea and we indulged in it. Our work there lasted several months, including a time when the Canadian Air Force occupied the quarters.

The only unusual event I recall about this period is when the chief British cook, a homosexual, broke into our tent in the dead of night. Jacab Laci was his target. We all threw the cook out of the tent.

We had no idea what happened to our families in Hungary. We were able to send cards but we never received any return mail. Many people boarded trains to Budapest. In the fall of 1945, we could not delay this trip any longer, and we were apprehensive about what we would find. I knew I was only going for a short visit regardless of the facts I would be facing. After surviving Nazi German occupation, it would be crazy to settle down under Russian occupation. Having spent considerable time with GI's, I felt strongly that the USA was the place for my future.

We spent days on the train, arriving in Budapest in the evening. Peter and I were fearful to confront potentially hideous facts so we did not leave the train before morning. I was heading to Vasvari Pal Utca where we used to have an apartment. When I reached the corner of Kiraly Utca, I was suddenly embraced by an old friend, Mellinger Jeno, who lived in our apartment building. He told me the fantastic news that my parents and sisters were in our old apartment.

A few minutes later, my family was in each others' arms. Thank God even my Wachtenheim grandma was with us. I was overwhelmed with happiness. My family had known I survived the war; they received one of my cards from Germany and were awaiting my arrival. Every member of my immediate family was in good shape, in good health. We were tremendously lucky!

My parents, sisters and I had a lot to discuss. We lived through many life-threatening events from 1944 to 1945. My Aunt Hedi and Uncle Leslie Fodor and their daughter Pimi survived in Budapest. So did my Uncle William Wachtenheim with Aunt Csopi. My Uncles Mor and Eugene Rabinek survived as did their wives.

Unfortunately, my favorite uncle, Leopold Rabinek, lost his life during the forced march toward Austria. My Aunt Melanie and Uncle Herman

Freund were deported from the city of Paks and murdered. Two of their sons, cousins Sandor and Ignac Freud, had perished.

My Uncle Bela Wachtenheim and family—his wife and three children who lived in Paris, France—survived by hiding. I never met anybody in that family. My other Uncle Eugene and Aunt Jeni, who lived in Paris with their four sons and a daughter, were deported by the Germans and murdered. We found documents regarding their deportation: Joseph and Salomon on 7/27/1942, Uncle Eugene, Desire and Michel on 8/3/1942, Aunt Jeni on 8/7/1942, and Madeline, the ten-year-old daughter on 8/24/1942. We had met Aunt Jeni and Madeline years earlier when they came to visit us in Hungary.

I was able to find and join a Zionist group planning to head to Germany as German Jews returning from Eastern Europe; thus we could cross borders. Before leaving Budapest, I spent time with some *gymnazium* schoolmates, including my friend Lowi Gyuri who survived the Mauthousen, Austria, concentration camp; his entire family was wiped out. Gyuri told me about many schoolmates who died in that camp.

After this short visit to my family, I boarded the train heading west. We had some problems crossing the Austrian border. We spent enjoyable days in Vienna. Continuing as displaced persons, we traveled through Salzburg, which had beautiful snow cover and we saw many horse-drawn sleds on the roads. Our trip ended in the British-occupied area of Germany at the Bergen Belsen Displaced Persons Camp. It was there I met my first girlfriend, Kandel Judit. Her parents were shot to death while sitting next to her. Who can remember all the tragedies?

Shortly after I settled in this camp, I looked for work and got an office job with the American Joint Distribution Committee (AJDC). My office handled requests by Jewish applicants to find their relatives living in the Western Hemisphere. Most countries in North and South America did not allow immigration unless a person applying had a citizen relative with whom they could join. I had adequate knowledge of English, German, and Hungarian languages to fill the requirements for the work.

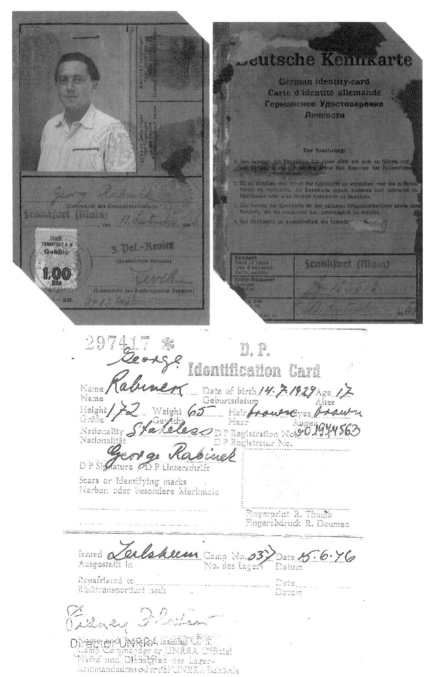

Our biggest problem was that the applicants, teenagers and many in their twenties, had only vague memories about the names and addresses of relatives. People came from all places in the British-occupied Germany to get our help. The one awful memory connected to this office was of a young Hungarian girl, my only coworker, who killed herself. I was unaware she was troubled or depressed.

There were a limited number of rooms so we had to share; Breznitz Joska was my roommate. We were not aware he had tuberculosis of the lungs and we shared smoking cigarettes. This must have been how I got TB.

Flori was the first girl with whom I had a relationship. But then my sister, Vera, arrived unexpectedly in the spring of 1946; still I was happy she joined me. She was so worn out she slept on and off for 24 hours the first day. I was amazed my parents let her come and that she found me, as we were not in touch. I got a room for both of us. Nobody had any furniture; we had a straw sack for a bed built on some empty gasoline cans.

While I worked, Vera joined groups of girls. The AJDC was helping the survivors in many ways. It provided clothing, education classes, and training classes for different skills. Vera, in the company of Polish and Lithuanian young people, tried the Yiddish language high school. But after a week of not understanding anything, she gave it up. Next she started going to a dental mechanics school taught by an American. This was fun for her as she always liked crafts. She hardly understood English and knew only a little Yiddish— the two languages used by the teacher. Baba, a friend, was with her in class. They often laughed at not understanding what was said. They were finally thrown out for disturbing the class.

Everyone in the displaced persons camp wanted to leave Germany. Most of these young people had survived against all odds, lost their families, and had no home to which they could return. Western European states did not open their doors, and Eastern Europe was still hostile and hateful to Jews. Vera and I wanted to start a new life in the United States. We were the pioneers of our family and our goal was to eventually be united with our parents and my other sister, Lili.

My office was the place where options for immigration were known, and required us to relocate to the U.S.-occupied section of Germany. The AJDC lined up an office job for me in Frankfurt am Main. Vera had friends in the DP camp so I could leave to find an apartment in the city (Spohr Strasse 40, owned by Fraú Becker).

My mind is hazy about the details of our life in Frankfurt. The most difficult problem I faced was getting a visa from the U.S. consulate. In the autumn of 1946, we started to apply for visas. My x-ray showed I had tuberculosis of the lung. I tried to solve this problem with a medical report from Hungary, which acknowledged I had TB more than ten years earlier and I had an arrested condition. The U.S. quota system, which was in force for many years, favored Germans. For other nationalities it would take a great many years to get a visa. It helped that we said we were born in Berlin.

Vera qualified for a children's visa, since we said we did not know if our parents were alive. I had to become younger to join her group. A few months after our first attempt, we renewed our application. Our apartment consisted of a single room with one bed, making us sleep head to foot. Later we were able to get an adjoining room, so we then had two bedrooms.

My daily life was so busy with work and solving problems that I was unaware of Vera's loneliness. We did not have acquaintances living nearby. Later we spent time with Hungarian-speaking DPs [displaced persons] like Schillinger Gyuri. We did not associate with Germans, though occasionally we talked to a few, like some relatives of Fraú Becker. The remarkably funny thing was that all Germans said the same thing to start: "I did not know of anything that happened."

Vera could not go to public school or work in my office. Lunchtime I could go to an officers' mess in my military-like uniform. Vera ate in our apartment. She remembers cooking dinners for us. I brought home rations like U.S. canned food. And we had German coupons, without which no food was available. Food was scarce.

Walking back and forth in Frankfurt was delightful for me as many sections of the city were in ruins due to English and U.S. bombings. On weekends we took walks along the Main River to the zoo and other points of interest. One of those times the police appeared in the park and asked for IDs. We did not have our papers with us. I was dressed in my American uniform and they let me be.

But they took Vera, loaded her into an open wagon with other women whom we suspected to be prostitutes, and took her to a police station. I walked home and back to the police with her papers. It was the middle of the night when I got her out. Vera remembers the police were verbally abusive and nasty to the women, which she found very funny. Every time the German authorities took a superior stand on morals, she experienced the irony.

Vera developed a high fever and Fraú Becker took care of her for a few days. Vera remembers that she washed and dried her, replacing her soaking wet pajamas after rinsing and drying them. This was a great kindness. Until then we did not have much to do with her.

Another time Vera had to be taken to a hospital with measles. Naturally I visited her daily. After a few days I got sick with measles. There was no way to communicate with each other as no phones were available. Vera had a difficult time finding me in a hospital. We both recovered in a short while, but I faced a tremendous problem: my TB was greatly reactivated. The AJDC arranged for me to go to a sanatorium where I spent a few weeks resting. Saul Trevin was my boss and he made sure I got what I needed.

I was resting in the company of Sajo Wohlberg, an ex-Hungarian, and a Russian named Kaidanov. I was worried about my next x-ray. I had to make sure it did not show any change as that would have indicated active TB. I was able to have a vacation in Berchtesgarden, a picturesque mountain village. Vera took the train to join me there. We enjoyed visiting mountains, lakes, hilltops, and the sights. On the other hand, the people in the tavern we visited were coarse in the way they talked and danced. It was a shocking contrast to the pure air and the lovely countryside. It was special for us to be together for a few days after all the troubled weeks.

My next x-ray looked exactly the same as the previous one. A short time later, after we received affidavits from a distant relative, Kertesz Miklos, we obtained our visas. We were taken by train to Hanover, a town in the northwest of Germany. After a few days, we arrived at Butzbach on the shore of the North Sea. On November 17, 1947, we boarded the SS *Ernie Pyle*, a small American ship. The night before boarding, I coughed up blood. I was in a dangerous situation and should have gone to a hospital. But I did not want to lose our visas so I took a chance. I would travel on the ocean, hoping the hemorrhage would not continue.

The passage took ten days and all that time I hardly moved. I got around extremely slowly. My lungs did not bleed during the boat trip. The boat was filled with young immigrants who started the trip happy and were running around. A few days later they were seasick and could not eat. They looked green and miserable. Vera and I were not affected by the motion of the boat and could eat as much as we desired. We had heaps of desserts until the ship's management started to put less food on the tables. There was a large group of young German women on our ship who were married to GI's. In the early evenings it was quite a sight to see them sneak down to the crew's quarters.

Finally, after crossing the astonishingly beautiful ocean, we arrived in the United States. The Statue of Liberty welcomed us as we approached New York City; seeing it touched us deeply.

When we arrived in New York, the Jewish Children's and Family Bureau took care of us for a couple days. I landed in a TB hospital in Denver, Colorado.

[Gyuri remained in the Denver hospital for three years. At the conclusion of his stay, he moved to Baltimore, Maryland where his sister Vera resided. A well-to-do family was fostering her, but she subsequently left to attend Brandeis University. Within a short period of time, Gyuri had another TB flare-up and was admitted to a Baltimore hospital. After his discharge, he married his first wife Helen. Gyuri studied architectural drafting and then enrolled in Johns Hopkins University to become an architectural designer. After nineteen years of marriage, Helen and Gyuri divorced.]

*My Early Impression of Gyuri*

I grabbed my jacket, he grabbed my arm, and we stepped outside to the waiting vehicle. He opened the passenger side door and I slid into my seat. A grinding noise emanated from the car and we accelerated slowly.

*Amadeus* is a beautiful film—comedic and memorable. We laughed often, leaning in toward each other with occasional comments about the film. Afterward in a café with a three-piece band playing in the background, his attention was focused solely on me. "You seem to enjoy Mozart?" he said.

I do, so I nodded.

"Mozart is my favorite composer," he informed me.

"Why Mozart?"

"I find his music cheerful."

We talked, drank wine, and munched on delicious chocolate cake. And we danced to the strains of the trio's music. The conversation was stimulating and continuous. We laughed often too.

His rapt attention was flattering, his Hungarian accent appealing, and his swashbuckling good looks captivating. All three certainly aroused my attention—first impression, first attraction, first date equaled chemistry.

At that moment in time, I knew little about George…or Gyuri, his Hungarian name. Perhaps the mystery intrigued me. After a first date, I wanted more but days and weeks passed slowly, and the phone remained silent.

*It was only one meeting, one get together. I won't think about him. Besides, he probably has some strange flaw.* I consoled myself with these thoughts.

But sweeping him away was not easy. Thoughts of him continued to creep into my brain.

Six weeks after that one date, his voice with the rolled R's flowed once more through the phone. "Hello, Roberta. Good evening. This is George."

# Budapest Bliss—
## Before the Horror

Throughout our life together, Gyuri displayed courage, resilience, love, and hope. But he emphasized that when he was a slave of the Nazis, luck was the primary reason for his survival. Yet his admirable qualities are evident in his recollections of the horrific World War II years he endured.

Consequently I was curious about his early life in Budapest before the war—who and what molded the man I married. We were sitting at our home dining room table on a Friday evening and the room was dim, the candles flickering. I asked Gyuri to tell me about his childhood. He sat quietly contemplating his answer. I waited.

After several moments he began to speak in his slow deliberate tone. "My childhood was happy. My memories are vague, but there were joyful times."

After a long pause I asked, "How did you spend the Sabbath?"

"Saturdays were the best. I love Sabbath food. We visited the grandparents—it was a requirement out of respect. On Saturdays after services we walked to my grandparents. My grandfather Rabinek blessed us children. Then we sat at the table to enjoy a feast.

"My father's parents, the Rabineks, and the Wachtenheims, my mother's parents, lived a block and a half from our apartment in the center of Budapest, the Pest side. The Wachtenheims were not a wealthy family; money was scarce but they were kind people. The Rabineks were well-educated and well-off; money was plentiful. My grandfather Rabinek was highly respected in the community. He was held in high esteem. People sought his advice and opinions on a variety of matters. *Anu*, my mother, held the Rabineks in high regard."

I nodded affirmatively, for *Anu* (Helen) had related stories about her in-laws to me. She was impressed by her well-educated father-in-law and the family's high lifestyle. Her remarks to me reflected her feeling she "married-up" by marrying Andrew, Gyuri's father. Andrew attended medical school, a rare accomplishment for a young Jewish man in Hungarian society of that time. Andrew Rabinek was the only Jew admitted to the school. Later Gyuri would tell me about his father, *Apu*, and his distressing medical school experiences causing him to leave the university after his third year.

But for now, Gyuri continued with his Sabbath food recollections:

"*Anu* was an excellent cook and the Sabbath had special foods. My two sisters, Vera and Lili, and I loved to eat and the aromas in our home were unforgettable. Challah bread, Kugler cake, cookies from Gerbeaud's, poppy seed cakes, sholet, and food always spiced with paprika. The grandparents also always set an aromatic table with sholet (a casserole of smoked meat or chicken, beans, and paprika) and a display of different stews. There were many desserts too. I particularly loved the poppy seed cookies."

I smiled at Gyuri. Sometimes he brought home cakes with poppy seed for me. He was now a diabetic and would only take a taste. But we always had paprika on our pantry shelf—Hungarian paprika only! The Hungarians are famous for rich food and their culinary skills. Memories of the delicious tastes and aromas invariably brought a twinkle to Gyuri's eyes and a smile to his lips. But to my continual surprise, he also enjoyed my simple healthy meals.

Gyuri took a sip of his coffee and sat quietly. After several moments, I said, "Your mother often said you were an excellent student who knew as much as any rabbi."

Gyuri smiled. "My sisters and I attended Jewish schools. Starting in the 1920s, Hungary had passed laws limiting Jews in professional positions. Many parents sent their children to Jewish schools where the education was superb. The *gymnazium* was the secondary school—the high school. The teachers were Jewish, fantastic professors who were not permitted to teach in the universities.

Since elementary school I studied German, Latin, and Hebrew. Later I studied English. It was a rigid academic schedule. Every day in the *gymnazium* we attended morning prayer services, and Sabbath services on Saturday. There was no school on the Sabbath, but we did go to school on Sundays."

"Was there time for friends, fun, and athletics?" I asked.

"Yes. I walked with several guys to and from the *gymnazium*. Usually a bunch of us played soccer in a park on the way home; we became inseparable. I was a fairly good soccer player and had many friends.

"The *gymnazium* was a mile and a half from my home. All high school students wore a cap that identified the *gymnazium*. We guys never walked alone. The danger of anti-Semitic attacks was prevalent and it was safer to walk in the group. Hordes of hateful kids pushed, threw stones, and caused riots.

"The girls attended a separate secondary school and interaction between the sexes was not encouraged. The restrictions for intermingling were rigid and expectations for academic success were high. The education was to prepare us to have more opportunities for a successful lifestyle. The theory was girls were a distraction. Anti-Jewish laws made career choices a difficult task. Yet I enjoyed the challenge of the academics."

Gyuri stopped speaking for a while, took another sip of coffee, and leaned back in his chair.

Again I interrupted his silence. "We have several of your paintings on our walls. Was art something you enjoyed in your youth?"

"A teacher at the *gymnazium* told me one day I may pursue art as a career."

"Architecture and art are twins, so you are now an architect," I commented. "But you no longer paint. Why?"

"Painting is time-consuming. I don't have time." Gyuri did not elaborate.

"What was family life about in Budapest?" I asked next.

"Our Budapest neighborhood had no trees; it was all paved. On weekends we took a streetcar far out on the Buda side of Budapest. It was hilly, and we could hike and enjoy the open air among the trees.

"In the summer we enjoyed family trips. The entire summer we spent at Lake Balaton. Sometimes a good friend of mine came to the lake with us. We did lots of swimming and the lake had a sandy shore. *Apu*, my father, remained at home as he had to work. He was a salesman and had a dry goods store. It was not his chosen career for *Apu* had a strong desire to be a physician.

"In the dry goods store he worked long hours. But on the weekends he visited us at the lake. He arrived on Friday, took a dip, and then we went to the synagogue services."

"Aside from the family life, what was life like in Hungary?" I prompted.

"It was a peaceful family life. My parents were protective and loving. But I knew of anti-Semitism since early childhood. Gangs—other high school guys—hurled rocks and clubbed the students from the Jewish gymnasium. It wasn't safe and we never walked alone! There was no protection from the anti-Semitic attacks.

"Stores had signs 'no Jews or dogs allowed' and Christmas was a dreaded holiday for Jews. The atmosphere was tense with hatred openly expressed and rampant. It was not a safe time or place. Laws restricting Jews from professions, businesses, and from certain neighborhoods were common. We were Jewish living in an anti-Semitic country.

"But before World War II, an influential and large Jewish community lived in Hungary. Some Jews even integrated and assimilated with the Hungarians. My family and I strolled along the Danube on Sundays. We wore typical clothing and appeared as any other Hungarian citizens. We didn't want to draw attention—that's what my parents taught us.

"But quotas for Jews in non-Jewish schools existed. My father's acceptance into medical school was a huge academic honor. Yet he was taunted in the university. He was called 'a stinking Jew' and often mocked for not writing on the Sabbath. Anti-Semitic gangs attacked him. When *Anu* heard of this, she summoned her group of girlfriends to help shield him from an attack. They came to the university, formed a circle around *Apu*, and shamed the anti-Semitic students. My *Apu* was saved from being badly beaten.

"Still the attacks continued and the taunting was relentless. Finally he had enough. In his third year my father left the university." Gyuri shook his head and murmured, "I felt he should not have given up."

Gyuri's feelings did not surprise me, though his father's fear to me was understandable. Earlier Gyuri had told me when the Nazis entered Hungary in 1944, he obtained a Christian birth certificate. I don't know how he managed this. He was convinced assuming another identity would save him. He hid the identity papers in his bedroom. His father located the certificate and burned it. Gyuri was furious.

He took the last sip of his coffee and placed the cup on the table, sitting without speaking while the candles dimmed.

The following evening we were having dinner in a quiet restaurant. Afterward Gyuri lingered over a second cup of coffee and began more of his recollections. "At a certain point, the Hungarian parliament started passing additional anti-Jewish laws. The non-Jewish clergy held powerful positions in the parliament but made no objection to these laws.

"On March 19, 1944, the Nazis occupied Hungary and on that day my childhood ended. We had no way of knowing of imminent danger. We did not often read the newspaper, for the newspapers were government owned. Tanks rolled into the street and students were directed to leave the schools and go home.

"I had completed my last year of studies and I had graduated. I was working in a factory. I wanted to go to a university but the anti-Jewish laws did not permit this. Once the Nazis took over, more laws against Jews were immediately issued. My job ended, my father lost his business, and we, the Jewish people, wore yellow stars on our outer clothing—that was the law.

"The horror story began."

*"Courage is resistance to fear, mastery of fear, not absence of fear."*—Mark Twain

*Questioning a Return*

"This came in the mail this morning," I said. Gyuri held his hand out to me. With a cursory glance at the paper, I added, "It's written in Hungarian. I have no idea what the letter says."

"Oh yes, sorry, I forgot to tell you," he said. "My old schoolmate from Budapest, Pista, sent the letter. I haven't spoken with him since the day the Nazis marched into Budapest."

"Is anything wrong?"

"No. He's asking if I want to attend our *gymnazium* reunion. I have no interest—it's a fascist nation, a dictatorship. After the war the Russians were not much better than Nazis—all murderous people."

"I know, but the communists have left. It's different now in Hungary," I added hesitantly.

"I left Hungary. I am an American now. The population was cruel. They stole from their neighbors who were slaves to the Nazis. And many collaborated with those Nazis. They leered gleefully at us prisoners who were marching to our deaths through the streets of Budapest. When the Russians occupied Hungary, the people were still consumed with hate."

"Yes, I understand. But now the communists have left. It will be different—a different Hungary."

"I left Hungary," he stated emphatically. "I bury the memories of them—the population of Budapest."

"But Gyuri, these are your boyhood friends," I coaxed, I reasoned, "your Jewish classmates who survived the war and the occupation. You will see them; you will hear about their lives today. And, it gives you an opportunity to come full circle, to see for yourself the end of the dictator regimes." Gyuri didn't respond but he reread the letter.

Several days later, he said, "I replied to the letter; let's book a flight. We are going to Budapest." This was 1992. Gyuri had left from Germany for the United States in 1947 on the ship the SS *Ernie Pyle*. From the moment he viewed the Statue of Liberty and first stepped foot on American soil, his dream was to be an American citizen. He no longer viewed himself as Hungarian. And he never expressed a desire to return to Europe, least of all to Hungary.

Throughout our marriage, when we traveled, we always toured the United States. Now we were going to Hungary, at my prompting.

# Visiting Budapest

On a Tuesday afternoon in May 1992, approximately 16 hours after our departure, Gyuri and I landed in Budapest. Pista, Gyuri's childhood friend—a tall, affable, sixtyish Hungarian gentleman—greeted us. Although his English was quite limited, his warm constant smile gave me a comfortable feeling.

Gyuri and Pista spoke Hungarian incessantly, despite their forty year separation. My first impression of the city included narrow streets crowded with zig-zag parked autos, old-world architecture, and drab gray buildings with worn fronts and falling plaster.

The next day, after a stroll toward the Danube River, we found a restaurant serving omelets and small food stores with an abundance of breads, jams, cakes and fruit. Then Pista rejoined us and we toured three synagogues.

First on the itinerary was Dohany Templon [temple]—impressive with wrought-iron fixtures, stained glass windows, and high ceilings. Unfortunately reconstruction made it impossible for us to visit the grave of Gyuri's grandfather. In the courtyard adjacent to the synagogue stood the graceful silver sculpture of a weeping willow tree with names of Holocaust victims inscribed on each leaf. Gyuri's sister Vera had purchased a leaf as a memorial to their grandfather, but we were unable to locate that either.

Kazinski Orthodox Synagogue was our next stop. In an outside courtyard was a wrought-iron *chuppah*. The marriage of Gyuri's parents took place under that *chuppah*, as *Anyu*'s father—Gyuri's maternal grandfather—attended this synagogue. Although in need of repair, the remnants of a beautiful building filled with life captured my imagination.

The third synagogue, Rombach Templon, had an attractive, colorful front. However, it had been sold for secular use. A Jewish group was hoping to repurchase it to establish a Jewish museum.

Streetwise aptly describes Pista. During the Nazi regime, he escaped from a heavily guarded forced labor battalion and managed to live out the remainder of the war hiding in Budapest. He was married to Ibolya for more than 40 years. Despite the language barrier, her friendly personality made me feel close to her. They have seven grandchildren and their three sons are a source of pride—two are physicians and one is a landscape architect. They are also Pista's business partners in the ownership of apartment buildings.

We walked quite a bit and went over the Chain Bridge across the Danube. To get to the Royale Palace, on the top of a steep hill in Buda, we rode the Sikló, an enclosed cable-like car pulled by a thick rope along a track. World War II bombings exposed portions of the ancient palace. I fell asleep at night dreaming of mysterious meetings and chocolate tortes like the ones in the fabulous dessert emporium, Gerbeaud, where we ate earlier. Gerbeaud survived the war intact and was thus reminiscent of pre-war Budapest.

The next day we walked to Kiraly (King's) Street. Although a drab gray area with narrow streets and buildings badly in need of repair, everything was amazingly clean and clear of debris. Vasvary Pal. Uta—the street where Gyuri and his family lived—was at first unrecognizable to him. Since the communists left, street names were changed too. Some signs held two street names.

A rather shabby temple, with only a single section in use for prayer meetings, was the site of Gyuri's Bar Mitzvah. Our next visit was to the apartment of his maternal grandparents and it was also deteriorated. We walked through a courtyard and an old Hungarian woman began talking to us in a disjointed manner. She pointed out the bullet holes in the building, but we didn't know if they were the result of World War II or the communist regime.

Later we pause on Raoul Wallenberg Street to take a snapshot and remember this hero. From the many wartime movies, books, and stories told, I could feel the presence of the Jews in the ghetto. I could only imagine Gyuri's feelings as we wandered through the area. He was silent about his reactions, for he wanted to absorb his emotions while we were on the trip; there would be plenty of time to talk back home. And he wanted me to have a good time and not be burdened by dark memories.

We met George and Eva Kertesz at a restaurant for dinner. Gyuri knew George from the *gymnazium* and the men had an enthusiastic, rapid exchange of conversation. Eva said to me, "Sit near me." Her English was slow, deliberate, correct, and without any recognizable Hungarian accent. For an hour and a half the four of us chatted and sipped our cooling coffee, and no waiter appeared interested in serving food. In a rush of Hungarian, there was a change of plans. Dinner would be served at their apartment; we took a brief ride on the Metro to a project-like development.

An iron gate enclosed their modest apartment. We entered a living room crammed with green plants and bulky furniture. A photograph of an extremely handsome man hung on the wall. The room reflected their love of flowers, plants, and books. Over a meager but attractively served sardine dinner, Eva described the cramped living quarters under the communist rule. Realizing they had no choice where to live or with whom to live was heartbreaking. Life had been hard and was still not a walk on easy street.

After dinner, which ended with tea, Eva and I wandered into a closet-like library. A picture of Jesus Christ was on the wall over the doorway. I asked a question that changed the entire mood of our conversation, "Who is that handsome young man in the picture—the picture in the other room?"

"My father. He died when I was 14," Eva answered. Then hesitantly she asked, "Are you a Jewish woman? You do not appear to be." After assuring her I was born into the Jewish faith—not converted because of Gyuri—she elaborated, "My father was a wise man. When he saw a man from Poland hiding in Budapest, my father's logic was when Hitler entered Hungary no Jew would be safe. He went to a cemetery, located a dead person's grave, and established the deceased's identity. As a lawyer, he was able to obtain Christian papers and move to another area of Budapest.

"A Christian physician neighbor schooled him about a childhood disease that would cause the need for circumcision. My father told my mother never to confess to being a Jew as he, under the most difficult torturous conditions, would never admit to Jewish identity. This lesson was instilled in me. I was devoted to my parents and listened well. I was to think of myself as Roman Catholic. There never would be any reason to confess to a Jewish identity. I never was Jewish. Like an actress, I assumed and believed the role.

"Hitler entered Hungary. Five neighborhood families were chosen for questioning. We were included. My father was questioned separately, my mother and I together. My memory is of my body shaking and my mother stroking me in a calming way.

"'Don't worry—the colonel is a nice man,' said one of the young Hungarian soldiers. 'He only dislikes Jews.'

"When my mother was told her husband confessed, she should confess and it would be an easier death, she reacted with innocence and would not comply. I, too, stated I was Roman Catholic. I had my period and was hiding sanitary cotton in my dress pocket. Two soldiers with guns aimed threateningly demanded I reveal the hidden item in my pocket.

"In childish anger, I threw the cotton onto the table, and the young soldiers surprisingly turned their heads in embarrassment. My parents and I were released. The other families were executed." I asked Eva how her father died, but she did not reply. She did say her mother died two years earlier at the age of 85. She attributed her mother's death to stress caused by the communist command that the family leave their old apartment and move to compact living quarters with strangers.

The next day the weather was gorgeous. We went to Margaret Island, a park with delightful attractions. The Olympic pool and mineral baths of Gyuri's childhood were still there. So were the long twisted paths through a wooded area, benches along the way, and people who were sitting on the grass. Even a topless female sunbather added to the entertainment.

A beautiful hotel with an outdoor restaurant overlooking the Danube enticed us. Lunch was elegant—an ample fresh salad, fine Hungarian wine, attentive waiters, handsomely dressed patrons, and a slight breeze. I felt like a princess.

In the late afternoon, Pista and his wife, Ibolya, drove us to the art colony town of Szentendre. We climbed numerous steps to a church overlooking the town. A Greek Orthodox Church, impressive with its walls covered with gilded gold icons, was another stop. We were struck by the contrast of the churches to the Jewish temples. The churches had no falling plaster and no signs of needed repairs or construction.

The reunion was the following day. With camera in hand, we took the Metro to our meeting place—Hotel Platanus. Pista concluded his introductory speech and everyone began to converse. Listening to several brief speeches and self-introductory updates in Hungarian gave me absolutely no insight into the program or the people attending the reunion. However, when Gyuri spoke, Eva translated the portion on our marriage and his two new daughters—my daughters. Afterward, I interacted with English-speaking attendees or depended upon an interpreter.

The few women who attended were open, friendly, and intelligent, and some of them spoke English. Cameras were clicking constantly.

From the hotel, we trekked to the *gymnazium* for a look at the old school. Because of overt anti-Semitism in Hungary before the war, Jewish students were forced to attend the exclusively Jewish school, but this law had its advantages. Jewish instructors were not accepted as professors in the universities, so the *gymnazium* benefited by having super teachers.

The massive building with its immaculate corridors was in excellent condition—in contrast to the Bar Mitzvah synagogue. In my imagination, I expected a less impressive structure. Instead I found the European architecture I love with its ornate friezes, high ceilings, marble, and polished wooden desks. Gyuri pointed out the spot where students and former students successfully defended the school from an attack by an anti-Semitic group.

A feeling of solidarity surrounded the group as we ambled through the corridors and in and out of classrooms. The alumni, still living in Hungary, never spoke of their Judaism or practiced it overtly after war. And they apparently never interacted with one another until this reunion.

Reaction to the reunion itself, however, was ambivalence. A lack of proper planning, food, and ample time to converse with friends was a disappointment to those who traveled the Atlantic Ocean for the occasion. But the feeling was—we came, we are connected. And that, after all, was the bottom line.

Our last day, we met Gyuri's cousin Trudy and her husband, George at a hotel for coffee and sinfully rich desserts. The couple gallantly attempted to include me but translating became burdensome. Since the conversation centered on relatives and the past, I politely asked to be excused to tour the hotel and gift shop.

To prolong our meeting, we strolled the streets of Budapest with them. They seemed to enjoy the conversation with Gyuri and I found them charming, despite the language barrier.

Strolling along the Danube, seeing the city illuminated by all the lights, chatting amiably and listening to Gyuri's animated conversation with people from his past, remains a happy memory for me.

Back in the United States, as we approach our tree-lined neighborhood, I ask Gyuri, "Any nostalgic feelings, regrets about leaving friends, the Hungarian language, and your childhood in Hungary?" He replies with shake of his head, a smile, and a look of inner peace. God Bless America. We are home.

# After the Trip to Hungary

Our visit was life-changing. I'm writing this years after our return from the trip we took in 1992 to visit Budapest. Hungary was the land of my husband Gyuri's birth—a country where he experienced hate, anti-Semitism, and murder.

The Nazis had a tranquil conscience about killing and maiming millions. Gyuri had gone through a time of hell. And he knew the communist conquerors were also a brutal dictatorship. So he sought freedom in the United States. Yet, for decades he remained silent about his time of imprisonment and the horrors he endured in concentration camps. He attempted to push life under a fascist regime to the recesses of his mind.

In America he got married, became an architect, and had three children. Nineteen years later he was divorced. In 1986 Gyuri and I married and blended our families. He spoke to me about his life during the war and gave his children an idea of his horrific experiences when they were age appropriate to understand. But life went on—he never discussed the past with others. A sad silence enveloped him.

A metamorphosis began one month after our 1992 journey to Gyuri's boyhood homeland. Perhaps one could call it a new beginning. Gyuri blossomed.

A few months after our plane landed back in Baltimore, my husband announced, "Roberta, I contacted the Jewish Council. I will become a Holocaust remembrance speaker."

Gyuri was prepared to tell the world about the horrors he endured under the fascist regime. And he did. His silence ended.

In the subsequent years until his death in 2014, Gyuri gave numerous talks to high school students, church members, synagogue congregations, social groups, and even a United States Army unit. He mentored individual high school students who were studying the Holocaust. Goucher College's students spoke to him and then performed a play based on his life. In addition, the Steven Spielberg Shoah Foundation interviewed and filmed him.

Often I was fortunate to accompany Gyuri to his speaking engagements where his talks were articulate and emotionally heartbreaking—his facts accurate and the audiences riveted. Positive reactions and follow-up letters of appreciation were moving to Gyuri.

His purpose was to ensure hate, bigotry, and cruelty in any form and directed toward any race, religion, or individual would never again occur. His theme was—no one should be a bystander—no one should remain silent in the face of brutality or bullying. For those who do not speak or act to condemn this are also guilty.

*Remembering Anu,*
*My Mother-In-Law*

I walk into her apartment. There is the warm aroma of a cooking pot and the sound of laughter. And there is a birthday cake on the table for Corinne, the first great grandchild who is having her first birthday. Gyuri and *Anu*'s granddaughter Sue are there as *Anu* bustles around filling my plate with an enormous slice of cake. Her giving food is part of my memory of *Anu*.

Months later, at predawn, Gyuri and I are called to her apartment. She felt ill and is lying across the bed, eyes fixed on the TV as someone is repeating words—a carefully slow and deliberate pronunciation—her daily English lesson. The ambulance is on its way.

I soon realize "tenacity" is *Anu*'s middle name. At the hospital there are many doctors and tests but no diagnosis and more tests are scheduled. But *Anu* has an invitation to her grandson Neil's wedding in California. She and I are alone in the dimly lit room. Her voice cuts the quiet. "I check out myself. I go to California. I don't need any more tests." *Anu*, Gyuri, and I are on a plane to California the next day.

It is difficult for me in California—my first meeting with the entire family and there are so many of them. With a glass in one hand and a plate in the other, I saunter through the crowd. I don't know if I am dressed properly for a California wedding and I really don't know anyone in the room. Suddenly *Anu*'s heavily accented voice is behind me, "You are the most elegant woman in the room." Perhaps I am dressed a bit too elegantly for a daytime California wedding. But at that moment, I begin to enjoy the reception.

Another time we are headed for New York on a train, the three of us, for the funeral of *Anu*'s brother-in-law. *Anu* chooses to sit next to me. An older man with a long straggly ponytail, and a voluptuous, oddly attired younger woman, are cuddling in a nearby seat. *Anu* makes conjectures about their lifestyle as I am a receptive audience to such harmless gossip. *Anu* likes this interaction in the company of other women.

Occasionally *Anu* and I go to a lovely restaurant for lunch with shopping afterwards. On one particular day, we view racks of designer dresses in Saks Fifth Avenue. A black sheath catches my eye and *Anu* wants me to try it on. "It would look good on your figure," she says. I quote the far-too-expensive price. With a twinkle in her eye and not a moment's hesitation, she replies, "Put it on Gyuri's charge account." We link arms, laugh, and walk out of the store empty-handed.

We are in Connecticut for her grandson David's wedding day. *Anu* and I sit alone at a table in the hotel lobby. She begins to recount memories of the war…her sisters…her nephews…a lost family. She speaks of her youth and happy times mixed with the horrid memories. She never mentions her own intrepidity; I only know about her bravery and devotion to family from Gyuri.

Nevertheless, her spunk is no revelation. *Anu* is tenacious, tough, willful, formidable. Her face reveals her tragedies, disappointments, and loneliness. Yet underneath it all is humor, laughter, devotion, and that enormous will.

With kisses,

Roberta

*Liberation Day*

My letter to Gyuri, dated May 4, 2006:

*Gyuri dear—we are shaped by those whom we love. On this day, I want you to know of my hope this is true for me. I hope I have been shaped by your strength, courage, depth, and integrity. So on this day, the anniversary of your liberation, I give myself credit for the insight I had to recognize you as a man of character. That perception began on the evening we spent hours in a restaurant—the night you spoke about your horrific experience.*

*It is not what you told me but how you told me. Through our twenty years together, your strength has shown like a beacon for me.*

*I love celebrating with you and I love you.*

*Roberta*

*Remembered*

Gyuri and I married January 11, 1986. His two sons, David and Robert, his daughter Sue, and my two daughters, Mauria and Rina, meshed well. Our family grew with marriages and eight grandchildren. Gyuri found a love of life with his architectural designs, extensive reading, learning study groups, and as an aquarium lecturer and guide. His life was full and he had a sense of rebirth. But underneath it all was always the darkness.

To expose that darkness to the light, Gyuri related his story to school children, adults, and to a group of U.S. Army soldiers. His legacy was to inspire others not to accept bullying, tyranny, or prejudice, and to not stand idle but to actively protest injustice.

Gyuri Rabinek died on August 29, 2014. We had 28 years of married life together. Before Gyuri's death, Steven Spielberg's Shoah Foundation interviewed and filmed him at our home and his story can be viewed at the Holocaust Museum in Washington, DC. The Holocaust Survivor Oral Histories of Goucher College in Baltimore, Maryland, also has an interview with Gyuri on file.

*Legacy*

After Gyuri's death, I made a decision. I wanted to continue his legacy, so I needed to talk about the Holocaust. I needed to deliver his message.

The Golden Door Organization sponsors people from all over the world who have settled in the United States. The immigrants are recruited to relate their experiences to schools and other groups. Most of these newcomers to our country have overcome unbelievable ordeals.

I wanted to tell Gyuri's story and the Golden Door Organization was the perfect vehicle. I contacted the director, and she was excited to mentor me. I became a storyteller about Gyuri's life under Nazi rule and my talks were directed to high school seniors. During my presentations, I emphasized Gyuri's age when he was arrested into a forced labor march. At that time, he was the same age as members of my audiences.

My purpose, as Gyuri's had been, was to tell a riveting story about the results of hate, bullying and bigotry—murder and destruction. I also sought to implore others to never be silent bystanders of hate.

This theme of "never again" continues to resonate through Gyuri's grandchildren, all of whom have been affected by his life story and the way he lived, and all are committed to his memory—Corinne, Rachel, Adam, Rebecca, Melissa, Samantha, Emily, and Andrew.

When they were old enough to understand, Gyuri spoke to each of our grandchildren and to my dear friend Adele's grandchildren, about his experiences. He was invited to Corinne and Rachel's high school classes to speak about the Holocaust too, creating a proud and memorable experience for them.

A high school teacher, Corinne presents lessons to her students about the Holocaust. She emphasizes history with the telling of her grandfather's story.

Rebecca is a high school English as a second or foreign language (ESOL) instructor. She teaches her students about the Holocaust using Elie Wiesel's book *Night* and the film, *The Pianist*, personalizing the curriculum with her grandfather's story.

Five of Gyuri's grandchildren—Adam, Corinne, Samantha, Emily, and Andrew—have traveled to Israel and were moved by their experience.

*And to all of the grandchildren, his life story, strength, energy, and will for freedom, are a continual inspiration.*

# The Children's Thoughts

These are notes my daughters, Mauria and Rina, wrote about their memories of Gyuri.

**From Rina:**

I remember George, my stepdad, leaving his voice message. "This is George from Baltimore," he said precisely, with his accented roll of the r's. But one could never recognize George's insight, dry humor or character from an initial meeting. It took a while to fully appreciate my stepdad. He was honest, precise, and inquisitive. And he was untiringly patient in answering any questions I posed to him.

I miss George, not because he was accessible like Google, but because he never failed to be there for me. He always wanted to talk to me, making me feel like an importance in his life.

He is unforgettable. I love and really miss him.

**From Mauria:**

George married my mom when I was 25 years old. Of course, I was thrilled she found someone with whom to share her life. But I was planning my own wedding, starting a new job, and not paying much attention to her new life. Over the years, I learned so much more about George and developed several wonderful memories.

- Coming to the hospital to take baby pictures of my daughter so I'd have memories from her first moments of life.

- My kids' excitement of the "nature walks" they went on with Grandpa, their plastic grocery bags full of treasures from the walks (leaves and acorns).

- His reaction of happiness and appreciation when I gave him a "goodie" basket full of all the snacks and foods he liked (the ones he deemed too expensive to buy for himself). It took years for me to realize he wasn't a man for whom you'd buy a Father's Day shirt or tie.

- His help planning my mom's surprise 70th birthday party. George basically told me to do anything I wanted—he was agreeable and excited for the celebration, and he wanted to pay for everything.

- His much-loved bike rides with the Baltimore Bike Club.

- The aquarium and his genuine enthusiasm for teaching all the kids about the first and exotic species of frogs, etc.

However, the memory that stands out the most for me is George's humor. I used to say to my mom, "Does anyone else realize how funny George is?" He would subtly and nonchalantly make comments that were hysterical. You had to really listen to catch them. I just loved that about him—he was never that serious.

In the almost 30 years that George was married to my mom, he never once said an unkind word to me, got angry, or "put me in my place," even when maybe he should have…. He was always helpful, respectful, supportive and just there for me and all of us—usually with camera in hand.

**This is from a conversation I had with Gyuri's son, David:**

"Every time the family meets at your home, I stare at the scenic oil painting on your dining room wall. Memories of Dad pop into my head."

David's observation did not surprise me. Yet I asked why these thoughts came to his mind.

"I think about our numerous camping trips, seaside vacations, and our walks through the woods. We talked and exchanged ideas. I like to remember my dad this way."

David hesitated for a moment before continuing. "Over the years I've introduced my son, Andrew, to outdoor pastimes. We have a close father-son relationship. Perhaps this is one major reason."

"Do you have any other recollections?" I asked.

"I thought my dad was an incredible man of substance. Our Seders were particularly memorable. He would step away from the traditional words of the Haggadah—the text read on the first two nights of Passover. And it became a personal, unique time. He reminded all of us around the table to count our blessings. We had freedom and we needed to cherish it. Also, he spoke of the tragedies—slavery, hate, and bigotry. He brought the younger family members the moving story of Anne Frank."

"Do you recall who sat at our Seder table?"

"Yes. Our Passover nights included an eclectic group—Jews and non-Jews. Everyone participated. Dad never lived life on the surface. He was not a man of small talk, but an inspiring teacher and a man who listened."

**This is from a conversation with Gyuri's son, Robert:**

The impression of Budapest, city of "The Blue Danube," in Robert's memory is a place marred by the atrocities of the Holocaust. As a young child, Robert and his father, Gyuri, were frequent visitors to Robert's grandmother Anu's apartment. Conversations about Holocaust experiences frequently dominated the visits, so they are vivid in Robert's memory. Years of devastation and horror under Nazi occupation seemed to Robert an integral part of Gyuri and Anu. The Holocaust hung in the air surrounding the Rabinek family for years, shaping who they were.

I asked Robert if any childhood recollections of their visits were happy ones.

"Yes," he replied. "Budapest family vacations and other pleasant pre-war interactions were occasionally mentioned."

"Your grandmother was an excellent cook," I commented. "Many Hungarians are known for their culinary skills. Did you enjoy her food?"

"Definitely, especially the sweets—mostly the poppy seed cakes that were mouth-watering. I recall they were the best."

"During those visits were you close to your grandmother?" I asked. "I mean, were your feelings toward Anu positive ones?"

"I was drawn to Anu's extreme loneliness and felt sensitive to her needs. My impressions of unhappiness, and for her extreme craving for attention, affected me. Of course, my mother also had those needs. Consequently my role in life was shaped. I became a caretaker."

**This is from a conversation with Gyuri's daughter, Sue, about when her father finally shared his story with his children:**

"I was in my early twenties and my brothers were a few years younger."

Sue was answering my question, "When did your father share his World War II experiences with you?"

Gyuri's children were aware he survived the war after spending time as a prisoner in several concentration camps, and that he came to the United States to live a better life. Yet throughout their childhood he never spoke about the war years. And no one questioned him. On a bookshelf in their home were paperback books relating to the Nazi occupation of Hungary and the Holocaust. Gyuri encouraged his children to read these books and they did. But no one questioned their father. And he never spoke about the readings.

During high school, Sue had some limited instruction about the Holocaust and viewed a related film. The impact of the movie affected her. Yet she never expressed those feelings, nor did she ask questions of her father. And Gyuri did not offer any details or insight about his horrific recollections.

"After seeing the Holocaust film, Sue, did you need to know the facts to explain your dad's silence?" I asked.

"The household atmosphere was tense—my parents were divorcing. As a young woman, I was focused on leaving the house and meeting my friends. My brothers were also involved with their own lives and needed to be away from the contention. We siblings did not discuss Dad's personal memories or the war years."

After the divorce, Gyuri moved to an apartment. The children's impression of him was of a strong man, knowledgeable, and taciturn—a survivor, tough, and capable. Gyuri believed his children—college educated and mature—were now ready to hear about the suffering he endured, and to learn about the cruelty of the Nazis and the millions they murdered. So he invited them to the apartment and spoke for hours about his horrifying memories.

The three siblings, stunned and upset hearing about the Nazi savagery, remained silent. No one asked a question. Sue envisioned her father as she recalled the Holocaust film she'd seen… as if smoke swirled around them. The stillness was deafening. Questions remained unspoken and unanswered for years to come.

*Reflection*

A loved one dies. The minutiae of life fades. And one finds time to reflect, to have a mirror into the departed's soul.

My husband Gyuri's memory never leaves my heart, but his inner struggles and experiences come unbidden to my mind's forefront.

Gyuri rose above the most horrific conditions and grew beyond them. He dealt with traumatic experiences, overcoming adversity to become an advocate for the rights of human beings.

His life story is my inspiration, compelling me to share its meaning with present and future generations.

# Acknowledgments

My first debt of gratitude is to my editor, Leslie Atkins, for her intelligence, resourcefulness, professionalism, and energy. I owe incalculable thanks to her insights.

Though my late husband's vision for a better world was the primary impetus for embarking on this book, another motivation was as a legacy for his children, his grandchildren, and for those in the future.

I owe appreciation to his children, Sue, David, and Robert, for their willingness to contribute to this book. And special thanks for spending hours with me on recollections about their father.

I am appreciative of our grandchildren and their significant others for technical support.

I credit my daughters, Mauria and Rina, for contributing memory letters about their stepfather and for their continual encouragement.

I appreciate our children's spouses—Sandy, Judy, Jeff, and Mike—for their sensitivity to Gyuri's story.

A special thanks to my friends for their steadfast support.

# *Glossary*

**Anu**—mother; mom (Hungarian)

**Appell**—roll call (German)

**Apu**—father; dad (Hungarian)

**Arrowcross**—Hungarian fascist organization

**Bar Mitzvah**—Jewish boy's 13th birthday religious ritual when he is first counted as an adult congregant

**Café Gerbeaud**—grand, high-ceilinged place to dine in Budapest, which serves coffee, cakes, and Hungarian bistro dishes

**Challah**—special bread for Sabbath and Jewish holidays

**Chuppah**—canopy beneath which Jewish marriage ceremonies are performed

**Concentration camps**—inadequate Nazi-run enclosed prison facilities used to persecute Jews and other minorities for forced labor or to await mass execution

**Ercsi**—small town south of Budapest in Hungary

**Fraú**—term of address for a married German woman

**Für die Juden**—for the Jews (German)

**Gymnazium**—secondary school in Europe that prepares pupils for university entrance (Hungarian)

**Häftlings**—slaves; inmates (German)

**Hatikvah**—19th century Jewish poem (meaning The Hope) and the national anthem of Israel

**Ja**—yes (German)

**Kapo**—inmate of Nazi concentration camp assigned to supervise other inmates (German)

**Kommandant**—commander (German)

**Kugler cake**—rich dessert cake (Hungarian)

**Raoul Wallenberg**—Swedish architect, businessman, diplomat,and humanitarian who saved thousands of Jews in Nazi-occupied Hungary (a fascist ally of Germany)

**Schutzpass**—protective document given by Raoul Wallenberg to every Jew who was able to apply for one or to Jews he located. It had the official seal of Sweden (a neutral nation during World War II).

**Sholet**—traditional Hungarian Jewish stew made with meat or chicken

**SS Ernie Pyle**—American transport ship used to bring displaced persons and refugees from Europe to the United States after World War II

**Templon**—temple; house of worship (Hungarian)

**Utca**—street (Hungarian)

**Wásser**—water (German)